*Personal Computer
Hardware Reference
Library*

S0-ATZ-213

BASIC HANDBOOK

General Programming Information

(Third edition – May, 1984)

The following paragraph does not apply to the United Kingdom or any country where such provisions are inconsistent with local law: International Business Machines Corporation provides this manual "as is," without warranty of any kind, either expressed or implied, including, but not limited to, the particular purpose. IBM may make improvements and/or changes in the product(s) and/or the program(s) described in this manual at any time.

This product could include technical inaccuracies or typographical errors. Changes are periodically made to the information herein; these changes will be incorporated in new editions of the publication.

It is possible that this material may contain reference to, or information about, IBM products (machines and programs), programming, or services that are not announced in your country. Such references or information must not be construed to mean that IBM intends to announce such IBM products, programming, or services in your country.

Products are not stocked at the address below. Requests for copies of this product and for technical information about the system should be made to your authorized IBM Personal Computer dealer.

The following paragraph applies only to the United States and Puerto Rico: A Reader's Comment Form is provided at the back of this publication. If the form has been removed, address comments to: IBM Corp., Personal Computer, P.O. Box 1328-C, Boca Raton, Florida 33432. IBM may use or distribute any of the information you supply in any way it believes appropriate without incurring any obligations whatever.

© Copyright International Business Machines Corporation 1982 1983 1984

Preface

The IBM Personal Computer offers three upwardly compatible versions of the BASIC interpreter: Cassette, Disk, and Advanced. This *BASIC Handbook* and the companion volume, the *BASIC Reference*, are references for these three versions of BASIC – and for the various releases of BASIC, beginning with 1.0.

It is important for you to know that these books are written *only as references* for the BASIC programming language, not as textbooks that will teach you how to program. If you need step-by-step instruction in learning to program in BASIC, we suggest that you ask for the materials you need at your library, bookstore, or computer store.

This book contains general information about using BASIC. There are sections that will help you get started using BASIC, and there are some sections that contain information on advanced subjects for the experienced programmer.

The *BASIC Reference* is an encyclopedia-type manual. It contains, in alphabetic order, the syntax and semantics of every command, statement, and function in BASIC.

These two BASIC books are extensively cross-referenced and indexed. Each also includes appendixes of useful information. In addition, there is a *Quick Reference* that lists all the BASIC commands, statements, and functions, categorized by task.

> **Note:** If you have an IBM PC*jr*, use the *BASIC* book specifically for the PC*jr* rather than these books.

The IBM Personal Computer BASIC Compiler is an optional software package that is available at your computer store. If you have the BASIC Compiler, use the IBM Personal Computer *BASIC Compiler* book in conjunction with this book and the *BASIC Reference*.

Related Publications

The following books contain related information that you may find useful:

- The IBM Personal Computer *Guide to Operations.*

- The IBM Personal Computer *Disk Operating System.*

- The IBM Personal Computer *Disk Operating System Technical Reference.*

- The IBM Personal Computer *Technical Reference.*

Summary of Changes

This summary first lists the changes that were made in BASIC release 2.∅, and then lists the BASIC release 3.∅ changes.

Changes in BASIC 2.0 and BASIC 2.1

The changes that were made in BASIC release 2.∅ are briefly described in the material that follows.

- Three enhancements were made to the BASIC command line:

  - The optional parameter *max blocksize* was added to the **/M:** switch, allowing you to reserve space beyond BASIC's data segment for assembly language subroutines.

  - The ATN, COS, EXP, LOG, SIN, SQR, and TAN functions now allow you to calculate in double precision by specifying **/D** in the BASIC command line.

  - You can redirect standard input and standard output by specifying <*stdin* or >*stdout* in the BASIC command line. *stdin* (redirect standard input) *stdout* (redirect standard output)

- Pressing Ctrl-PrtSc causes text sent to your screen to also be sent to your system printer.

- The *filespec* syntax was expanded to allow the specification of a path for a device or file. All commands and statements that accept *filespec* also accept *path*. The commands that allow paths are

BLOAD, BSAVE, KILL, LOAD, MERGE, NAME, RUN, and SAVE. The statements that allow paths are CHAIN and OPEN.

- The DELETE command syntax was expanded to allow line deletions from the specified line to the end of the program.

- The **PE** option was added to the OPEN "COM... statement syntax to allow for parity checking.

- The **PLAY** statement has two new options. (For use in Advanced BASIC only.)

    - $>n$ raises the octave and plays note n.

    - $<n$ lowers the octave and plays note n.

- The DRAW statement has two new options. (For use in Advanced BASIC only.)

    - **TA**(n) turns angle n from -36Ø to 36Ø degrees.

    - **P** *paint,boundary* sets figure color and border color.

- The POINT function allows the form **v=POINT(n)**, which returns the value of the current x or y graphics coordinate. (For use in Advanced BASIC only.)

- The RANDOMIZE statement allows double-precision expressions.

- The LINE statement has a new option, *style*, which uses hexadecimal values to plot a pattern of points on the screen. (For use in Advanced BASIC only.)

- The PAINT statement has a new feature, *tiling*, which allows you to paint an area with a pattern rather than just a solid color. (For use in Advanced BASIC only.)

- The ON KEY(n), KEY(n), and KEY statements now allow trapping of six additional definable keys, 15-2∅. (For use in Advanced BASIC only.)

- The GET and PUT statements were enhanced to allow record numbers in the range 1 to 16,777,215 to accommodate large files with short record lengths.

- EOF(∅) returns the end-of-file condition on standard input devices used with redirection of I/O.

- The LOF function returns the actual number of bytes allocated to a file.

- The graphics statements CIRCLE, DRAW, LINE, PAINT, POINT, PSET, PRESET, VIEW, and WINDOW now use line clipping instead of wraparound.

Three new functions were added:

- The PLAY(n) function returns the number of notes currently in the Music Background (MB) buffer. (For use in Advanced BASIC only.)

- The PMAP function maps an expression to world or physical coordinates. (For use in Advanced BASIC only.)

- The TIMER function returns the number of seconds that have elapsed since midnight or System Reset.

Four new statements were added:

- The ON PLAY statement allows continuous music to play while a program is running. (For use in Advanced BASIC only.)

- The ON TIMER statement transfers control to a given line number in a BASIC program when a defined period of time has elapsed. (For use in Advanced BASIC only.)

- The VIEW statement lets you define a viewport (or area) within the physical limits of the screen. (For use in Advanced BASIC only.)

- The WINDOW statement lets you redefine the coordinates of the screen or viewport. (For use in Advanced BASIC only.)

Three new commands were added:

- The CHDIR command allows you to change the current directory.

- The MKDIR command creates a directory on the specified disk.

- The RMDIR command removes a directory from the specified disk.

Changes in BASIC 3.0

The following changes have been made in BASIC release 3.∅:

- Device support allows BASIC to communicate with user-installed device drivers through the IOCTL statement and IOCTL$ function.

- IOCTL and IOCTL$ are used to get information to and from device channels.

- ENVIRON statement and ENVIRON$ function allow you to modify parameters in BASIC's environment table.

- ERDEV and ERDEV$ are device error variables that allow you to read INT 24 error codes.

- SHELL allows you to execute DOS commands and run child processes from BASIC.

  Note: The terms "disk," "diskette," and "fixed disk" are used throughout this book. Where "diskette" is used, it applies only to diskette drives and diskettes. Where "fixed disk" is used, it applies only to the IBM nonremovable fixed disk drive. Where "disk" is used, it applies to both fixed disks and diskettes.

Contents

Chapter 1. The Versions of BASIC

Contents

The Versions of BASIC

IBM offers three versions of the BASIC interpreter for the Personal Computer:

- Cassette
- Disk
- Advanced

The three versions of BASIC are upwardly compatible; that is, Disk BASIC does everything Cassette BASIC does, plus a little more, and Advanced BASIC does everything Disk BASIC does, plus a little more. The differences between the versions are discussed further on in this section.

All three versions of BASIC include these features:

- Extended character set. You can display 256 different characters— the usual letters, numbers, and symbols, plus international characters and other symbols such as Greek letters used in scientific and mathematical applications.

- Graphics capability. If you have the Color/Graphics Monitor Adapter, you can draw points, lines, and entire pictures. The screen is *all points addressable* in either medium or high resolution. See Chapter 3, as well as the *BASIC Reference*, for more information.

- Special input/output device support. You can use sound, a light pen, and joysticks, to make your programs more interesting and more fun.

The commands, statements, and functions for all three versions of BASIC are described in detail in the *BASIC Reference* manual. Included in each description is a "Versions" line that specifies the versions of BASIC that support the command, statement, or function.

For example, if you look under "CHAIN Statement" in the *BASIC Reference*, you will note that it says:

Versions:

Cassette	Disk	Advanced	Compiler
***	***		(**)

The asterisks show which versions of BASIC support the statement. This example shows that you can use the CHAIN statement for programs written in the Disk and Advanced versions of BASIC.

In this example you will notice that the asterisks under the word "Compiler" are in parentheses. This means that there are differences between the way the statement works under the BASIC interpreter and the way it works under the IBM Personal Computer BASIC Compiler. The IBM Personal Computer BASIC Compiler is an optional software package available from IBM. The *BASIC Compiler* manual explains these differences.

Cassette Basic

The nucleus of BASIC is the Cassette version, which is built into your IBM Personal Computer in 32K-bytes of read-only storage. You can use Cassette BASIC with any IBM Personal Computer, regardless of the amount of random access memory the computer has. The amount of storage you can use for programs and data depends on how much memory is in your Personal Computer. The number of "bytes free" is displayed after you switch on the computer.

The only storage device you can use to save Cassette BASIC information is a cassette tape recorder. You cannot use diskettes with Cassette BASIC.

Disk BASIC

This version of BASIC is a program on the IBM
Personal Computer Disk Operating System (DOS)
diskette. DOS is an IBM software product that is
available separately. You load Disk BASIC from the
DOS diskette before you use it. The amount of storage
you can use for programs and data is displayed on the
screen when you start BASIC.

Special features of Disk BASIC are:

* Input/output to disk in addition to cassette. See
  Appendix A for more information.

* An internal clock that keeps track of the date and
  time.

* Asynchronous communications (RS232) support.
  See Appendix C in the *BASIC Reference* for more
  information.

* Support for two additional (total of three) printers.

Advanced BASIC

Advanced BASIC is the most extensive form of BASIC
available for the IBM Personal Computer. Like Disk
BASIC, it is a program on the IBM DOS diskette, and
you must load into memory before you use it. As with
the other versions, the number of free bytes you have
for programs and data is displayed on the screen when
you start BASIC.

Key features found only in Advanced BASIC are:

- Event trapping. A program can respond to the occurrence of a specific event by "trapping" (automatically branching) to a specific program line. Events that can be trapped include: communications activity, a function key being pressed, the button being pressed on a joystick, play activity, timer activity and the light pen being activated.

- Advanced graphics. Additional statements (CIRCLE, DRAW, GET, PAINT, PMAP, POINT, PSET, PUT, VIEW, and WINDOW) make it easier to create complex graphics scenes.

- Advanced music support. The PLAY statement makes it easy to use the built-in speaker to create musical tones.

Chapter 2. How to Start and Use BASIC

Contents

Getting BASIC Started

It's easy to start BASIC on the IBM Personal Computer:

To Start Cassette BASIC

Important: Use Cassette BASIC only if you do not have any type of disk with your system. If you have a disk system, use Disk or Advanced BASIC.

If your computer is off:

Switch on the computer.

The words "Version C" and the release number are displayed along with the number of free bytes.

If your computer is on:

1. Make sure there is no diskette in drive A.

2. Press and hold down the Ctrl and Alt keys while you press the Del key.

The words "Version C" and the release number are displayed along with the number of free bytes.

To Start Disk BASIC

1. Insert the IBM DOS diskette into drive A.

2. Switch on the computer.

3. When you see the DOS prompt (A>), enter the command **BASIC**.

   The words "Version D" and the release number are displayed along with the number of free bytes.

To Start Advanced BASIC

1. Insert the IBM DOS diskette into drive A.

2. Switch on the computer.

3. When you see the DOS prompt (A>), enter the command **BASICA**

   The words "Version A" and the release number are displayed along with the number of free bytes.

Returning to DOS

At times you may want to return to DOS after running a BASIC program; for example, you may want to change from Disk BASIC to Advanced BASIC.

To return to DOS from BASIC:

1. When BASIC prompts you for a command, type:

   SYSTEM

   then press the Enter key.

2. When you see the DOS prompt, DOS is ready for you to give it a command.

For more information, see "SYSTEM Command" in the *BASIC Reference*.

Options in the BASIC Command Line

You can include options in the **BASIC** command line when you start Disk BASIC or Advanced BASIC. These options specify the amount of storage you want BASIC to use for programs and data, and for buffer areas. You can also tell BASIC to immediately load and run a program.

But these options are not required—BASIC works just fine without them. So if you're new to BASIC, you may wish to skip over this section, which has been written for experienced BASIC programmers, and go on to the section called "Modes of Operation." Then you can refer back to this section when you become more familiar with BASIC.

The complete format of the **BASIC** command is:

BASIC[A] [*filespec*] [<*stdin*] [>] [>*stdout*] [/F:*files*] [/S:*bsize*] [/C:*combuffer*] [/M:[*max workspace*] [,*max blocksize*]] [/D]

In this syntax, the following conventions are used:

- Words in capital letters are keywords and must be entered as shown, except that they may be entered in any combination of uppercase (capital letters) and lowercase (small letters). BASIC converts words to uppercase unless they are part of a quoted string, remark, or DATA statement.

- You must supply any items shown in lowercase italic letters.

- Items in square brackets ([]) are optional.

- An ellipsis (...) indicates that an item may be repeated as many times as you wish.

- All punctuation except square brackets (such as commas, parentheses, semicolons, hyphens, or equal signs) must be included where shown.

An explanation of the options follows.

filespec   This option names a program that is to be loaded and run immediately by BASIC. BASIC will proceed as if a RUN <*filename*> were given after initialization was complete. In BASIC 2.∅ and later releases, *filespec* is expanded to allow you to specify a path. It must conform to the rules for specifying files described in Chapter 3. A default extension of .BAS is used if none is given. This allows BASIC programs to be run in batch processing mode by putting this form of the command line in an AUTOEXEC.BAT file. Programs run in this manner should be exited with the SYSTEM command so that the next command for the AUTOEXEC.BAT file can be executed. Note that when you specify *filespec*, the BASIC heading with the copyright notices is not displayed.

<stdin

A BASIC program normally receives its input from the keyboard (standard input device). Using <*stdin* allows BASIC to receive input from a file you specify. When you use <*stdin*, you must place it before any switches in the command line. (A *switch* is an option beginning with a slash (/) that is used to specify parameters.) Refer to "Redirection of Standard Input and Output" later in this chapter for more information. (For use in BASIC 2.∅ and later releases.)

>stdout

A BASIC program normally writes its output to the screen (standard output device). Using >*stdout* allows BASIC to write output to a file or device you specify. When you use >*stdout*, you must place it before any switches in the command line. Refer to "Redirection of Standard Input and Output" later in this chapter for more information. (For use in BASIC 2.∅ and later releases.)

The following options in the BASIC command line are switches:

/F:files   This switch sets the maximum number of files that can be open at any one time during the running of a BASIC program. Each file requires 62 bytes of memory for the file control block (FCB), plus 128 bytes for the data buffer. The size of the data buffer can be altered with the /S: switch. If the /F: switch is omitted, the number of files defaults to 3. The actual number of files that can be open simultaneously depends upon the value of the FILES= parameter in the DOS configuration file, CONFIG.SYS. The maximum value for FILES= is 15. The default value for FILES= is 8. The first three file handles are taken by *stdin, stdout, stderr, stdaux,* and *stdprn.* One additional handle is needed by BASIC for LOAD, SAVE, CHAIN, NAME, and MERGE. So when FILES=1∅, 6 are left for BASIC file I/O. Thus /F:6 is the maximum to give when FILES=1∅ and you want to be able to have all files open at once.

If you attempt to OPEN a file after all the file handles have been exhausted, a **Too many files** error will result.

/S:bsize   This switch sets the buffer size for random files. The record length parameter on the OPEN statement cannot exceed this value. The default buffer size is 128 bytes. The maximum value you can enter is 32767 bytes.

/C:combuffer

This switch sets the size of the buffer for receiving data when you are using an Asynchronous Communications Adapter. This switch has no effect unless you have an Asynchronous Communications Card on your system. The buffer for transmitting data with communications is always allocated to 128 bytes. The maximum value you can enter for the /C: switch is 32767 bytes. If the /C: switch is omitted, 256 bytes are allocated for the receive buffer.

If you have a high-speed line, we suggest you use /C:1Ø24. If you have two Asynchronous Communications Adapters on your system, both receive buffers are set to the size specified by this switch. You can disable RS232 support by using a value of zero (/C:Ø), in which case no buffer space will be reserved for communications, and communications support will not be included when BASIC is loaded. Any subsequent communications I/O attempts will result in a **Device unavailable** error.

/M:max workspace

This switch sets the highest memory location that can be used by BASIC. BASIC will attempt to allocate 64K of memory for the data and stack segments. If you are going to use assembly language subroutines with BASIC, you can use the /M: switch in the BASIC command line.

For example, /**M:32768** allocates 32768 bytes for BASIC's data and stack segments and allows you to use the other 32768 bytes for assembly language routines if you wish. For more information, see the BASIC memory map in the section on calling assembly language subroutines from BASIC in Appendix B of the *BASIC Reference.*

:max blocksize

If you intend to load routines above the highest location that BASIC can address (65536), you should specify the option **max blocksize** to reserve space for them. This is necessary if you intend to use the SHELL statement. (For more information see "SHELL Statement" in the *BASIC Reference.*) Failure to use **max blocksize** could result in COMMAND.COM being loaded on top of your routines when a SHELL statement is executed.

The option **:max blocksize** specifies the maximum number of paragraphs allocated for BASIC, plus the space beyond the stack that you want to use for assembly language subroutines. Paragraphs are blocks of 16 bytes each. When **max blocksize** is omitted, &H1ØØØ (4Ø96) is assumed, and 65536 (4Ø96 * 16) bytes are allocated for BASIC's data and stack segments.

For example, if you want 65536 bytes for BASIC and 512 bytes for assembly language subroutines, then use /**M:,&H1Ø2Ø** (4Ø96 paragraphs for BASIC + 32 paragraphs for your routines).

/M:,2Ø48 tells BASIC to allocate and use 2Ø48 paragraphs (32768 bytes) for the data and stack segments.

/M:32ØØØ,2Ø48 says to allocate 32768 bytes maximum, but BASIC will use only the lower 32ØØØ. This leaves 768 (32768 - 32ØØØ) bytes reserved for your use. (For use in BASIC 2.Ø and later releases.)

/D

This switch causes the double-precision mathematics functions to remain resident. When you specify **/D**, approximately 3ØØØ additional bytes are resident in BASIC for use by the transcendental functions. The functions that can be converted to double precision are: ATN, COS, EXP, LOG, SIN, SQR, and TAN. If **/D** is omitted, the double-precision function is disregarded, and the space is freed for program use. (For use in BASIC 2.Ø and later releases.)

Note: The options *files, max workspace, max blocksize, bsize*, and *combuffer* can be expressed in decimal, octal (preceded by &O), or hexadecimal (preceded by &H).

Some examples of the BASIC command line:

BASIC PAYROLL

Uses 64K of memory and 3 files; loads and executes PAYROLL.BAS.

BASICA INVENT/F:6

Uses 64K of memory and 6 files; loads and executes INVENT.BAS. (You must change the CONFIG.SYS file to FILES=1Ø if you want to use 6 files.)

```
BASIC /C:0/M:32768
```

Disables RS232 support and uses only 32K of memory for BASIC workspace.

```
BASIC /F:4/S:512
```

Uses 4 files and allows a maximum record length of 512 bytes.

```
BASIC TTY/C:512
```

Uses 64K of memory and 3 files; allocates 512 bytes to RS232 receive buffers and 128 bytes to transmit buffers; loads and executes TTY.BAS.

Redirection of Standard Input and Output

In BASIC 2.∅ and later releases, you can redirect BASIC input and output. Standard input, normally read from the keyboard, can be redirected to any file you specify in the BASIC command line. Standard output, normally written to the screen, can be redirected to any file or device you specify in the BASIC command line.

BASIC *filespec* [<*stdin*] [>] [>*stdout*]

Notes:

- When redirected, all INPUT, INPUT$, INKEY$, and LINE INPUT statements read from the specified input file, instead of from the keyboard.

- When redirected for input *and* output, all PRINT statements and error messages write to the specified output file or device, instead of to the screen.

- When a file is redirected only for output, any data that appears on the screen will go to the specified output file.

- When only output is redirected, error messages go both to the screen and to the specified output file. All files are closed, the program ends, and control returns to DOS.

- File input from "KYBD:" is still read from the keyboard.

- File output to "SCRN:" still goes to the screen.

- BASIC continues to trap keys when an ON KEY(*n*) statement is specified.

- Ctrl-PrtSc does not give a printed copy of the screen when standard output is redirected.

- Ctrl-Break goes to standard output, closes all files, and returns control to DOS.

Some examples of redirection of I/O:

```
BASIC MYPROG >DATA.OUT
```

In the example above, data read by INPUT, INPUT$, INKEY$, and LINE INPUT will continue to come from the keyboard. All screen output will go into the DATA.OUT file. This includes all data printed to the screen with the PRINT statement, any error messages that BASIC prints to the screen, and any data entered in direct mode.

```
BASIC MYPROG <DATA.IN
```

Data read by INPUT, INPUT$, INKEY$, and LINE INPUT will come from the DATA.IN file. Data written by PRINT will continue to go to the screen.

```
BASIC MYPROG <MYINPUT.DAT >MYOUTPUT.DAT
```

Data read by INPUT, INPUT$, INKEY$, and LINE INPUT will come from the MYINPUT.DAT file and data written by PRINT will go into the MYOUTPUT.DAT file.

```
BASIC MYPROG <\SALES\JOHN\TRANS.>>\SALES\
SALES.DAT
```

Data read by INPUT, INPUT$, INKEY$, and LINE INPUT will come from the \SALES\JOHN\TRANS file. Data written by PRINT will be *appended* to the \SALES\SALES.DAT file.

Modes of Operation

Once BASIC is started and displays the prompt **Ok**, it is ready to receive instructions from you. This state is referred to as *command level.* You can communicate with BASIC in either of two modes: *direct mode* or *indirect mode.*

Direct Mode

In direct mode, you instruct BASIC to perform your request immediately after it is entered. You do this by omitting the line number from the the statement or command. You can display results of arithmetic and logical operations immediately or store them for later use, but the instructions are not saved after they are executed. This mode is useful for debugging as well as for quick computations that do not require a complete program. For example:

```
PRINT 20+2
 22
```

Indirect Mode

In indirect mode, you tell BASIC that the line you are entering is part of a program. To do this, you begin the line with a *line number.* The line is then stored as part of the program in memory. The stored program is executed by entering the RUN command. For example:

```
1 PRINT 20+2
RUN
 22
```

The Keyboard

The keyboard is divided into three general areas:

- Ten function keys, labeled F1 through F1∅, are on the left side of the keyboard.

- The "typewriter" area is in the middle. This is where you find the regular letter and number keys.

- The numeric keypad, similar to a calculator keyboard, is on the right side.

General use of the keyboard is described in the *Guide to Operations*. The following paragraphs describe specific keyboard use for BASIC.

Function Keys

The functions keys can be used:

- As "soft keys." That is, you can set each key to type automatically any sequence of of up to 15 characters. Some frequently used commands have already been assigned to these keys. You can change these if you wish. See "KEY Statement" in the *BASIC Reference* for details.

- As program interrupts in Advanced BASIC, through use of the ON KEY statement. See "ON KEY(n) Statement" in the *BASIC Reference*.

Special Key Combinations

The section that follows describes some key combinations that are available in BASIC.

ALT Key

You can use the ALT (Alternate) key to type an entire BASIC keyword with a single keystroke.

To do this, hold down the ALT key and press one of the alphabetic keys, A-Z. Keywords associated with the letters are listed below. Letters that do not have reserved words associated them are noted by "(no word)."

A	AUTO	O	OPEN
B	BSAVE	P	PRINT
C	COLOR	Q	(no word)
D	DELETE	R	RUN
E	ELSE	S	SCREEN
F	FOR	T	THEN
G	GOTO	U	USING
H	HEX$	V	VAL
I	INPUT	W	WIDTH
J	(no word)	X	XOR
K	KEY	Y	(no word)
L	LOCATE	Z	(no word)
M	MOTOR		
N	NEXT		

You can also use the ALT key with keys on the numeric keypad to enter characters not found on the keys. To do this, hold down the Alt key and type the three-digit ASCII code for the character. See Appendix D in the *BASIC Reference* for a complete list of ASCII codes.

Ctrl Key

The Ctrl key is also used to enter certain codes and characters not otherwise available from the keyboard.

For example, **Ctrl-G** is the *bell* character. When this character is printed, the speaker beeps. To enter the bell character, hold down the Ctrl key and press the G key.

Ctrl-Break

Ctrl-Break interrupts program execution at the next BASIC instruction and returns to BASIC command level. It is also used to exit the AUTO line numbering mode. To use Ctrl-Break, hold down the Ctrl key and press the Break key.

Ctrl-PrtSc

In BASIC 2.∅ and later releases, Ctrl-PrtSc can be used as an on/off switch to cause any text sent to the screen to be also sent to the printer. Press and hold the Ctrl key, press the PrtSc key, and then release both keys to print display output on the printer. Press and release both keys again to stop printing display output on the printer.

Although Ctrl-PrtSc allows the printer to function as a system log, it slows some operations because the computer does not continue until the printer stops.

Ctrl-PrtSc is disabled when an error condition occurs.

You also use the Ctrl key together with other keys when you edit programs with the BASIC program editor. These operations are explained in the section that follows.

The BASIC Program Editor

Any line of text typed while BASIC is at the command level is processed by the BASIC Program Editor. The Program Editor is a "screen line editor." That is, you can change any line on the screen, one line at a time. The change will take effect only when you press Enter on that line.

To become familiar with the capabilities of the Program Editor, enter a sample program and practice using the edit keys as described on the pages that follow.

Special Program Editor Keys

You can use keys on the numeric keypad, the Backspace key, and the Ctrl key to move the cursor (blinking underscore or box) to a location on the screen, insert characters, or delete characters.

Key(s)	Function
Home	Moves the cursor to the upper left-hand corner of the screen.
Ctrl-Home	Clears the screen and positions the cursor in the upper left-hand corner of the screen.
↑ **(Cursor Up)**	Moves the cursor up one line.
↓ **(Cursor Down)**	Moves the cursor down one line.

← **(Cursor Left)**	Moves the cursor left one position. If the cursor advances beyond the left edge of the screen, it moves to the right side of the screen on the preceding line.
→ **(Cursor Right)**	Moves the cursor right one position. If the cursor advances beyond the right edge of the screen, it moves to the left side of the screen on the next line down.
Ctrl → **(Next Word)**	Moves the cursor right to the next *word*. A *word* is any alphanumeric character or group of characters preceded by a blank or special character.

For example, in the following line:

```
LINE (L1,LOW2)-(MAX,48) ,3 , BF
```

the cursor is in the middle of the word **LOW2**. If you press Next Word (Ctrl-Cursor Right), the cursor moves to the beginning of the next word, which is **MAX**:

```
LINE (L1,LOW2)-(MAX,48) ,3 , BF
```

If you press Next Word again, the cursor moves to the next word, which is the number 48:

```
LINE (L1,LOW2)-(MAX,48) ,3 , BF
```

Ctrl ←
(Previous Word)   Moves the cursor left to the beginning of the previous word. The previous word is the letter or number to the left of the cursor that is preceded by a blank or special character.

For example, suppose you have:

```
LINE (L1,LOW2)-(MAX,48) ,3 , BF_
```

If you press Previous Word (Ctrl-Cursor Left), the cursor moves to the beginning of the word **BF**:

```
LINE (L1,LOW2)-(MAX,48) ,3 , BF
```

When you press Previous Word again, the cursor moves to the number 3:

```
LINE (L1,LOW2)-(MAX,48) ,3 , BF
```

End   Moves the cursor to the end of the logical line.

Ctrl-End   Erases to the the end of a logical line.

Ins   Sets insert mode on or off. In insert
mode, the cursor covers the lower
half of a character position.

When insert mode is on, characters
above and following the cursor move
to the right as characters are
inserted. Line wrapping occurs; that
is, as characters advance off the right
side of the screen they return on the
left of the next line.

When insert mode is off, any
characters typed replace the existing
characters on the line.

> **Note:** You can also turn off
> insert mode by pressing any of
> the cursor movement keys or the
> Enter key.

Del   Deletes the character at the current
cursor position. All characters to the
right of the deleted character move
one position left to fill in the empty
space. Line wrapping occurs; that is,
if a logical line (to the next Enter)
extends beyond one physical line,
characters on subsequent lines move
left one position to fill in the
previous space, and the character in
the first column of each subsequent
line moves up to the end of the
preceding line.

← **(Backspace)**	Deletes the last character typed. That is, it deletes the character to the left of the cursor. All characters to the right of the deleted character move left one position to fill in the space. Subsequent characters and lines within the current logical line move up as with the Del key.
Esc	When pressed anywhere in a line, erases the entire logical line from the screen. The line is not passed to BASIC for processing. However, if it is a program line (begins with a line number), it is not erased from the program in memory.
Ctrl-Break	Returns to command level *without* saving any changes that were made to the line being edited. It does not erase the line from the screen as Esc does.

→ |
(Tab)

Moves the cursor to the next tab stop. Tab stops occur every 8 character positions (1, 9, 17, and so on).

When insert mode is off, pressing the Tab key moves the cursor over characters until it reaches the next tab stop.

For example, suppose you have the following line:

```
10 REM this is a remark
```

If you press the Tab key, the cursor will move to the ninth position as shown:

```
10 REM this is a remark
```

When insert mode is on, pressing the Tab key inserts blanks from the current cursor position to the next tab stop. Line wrapping occurs as explained under **Ins**. For example, suppose you have this line:

```
10 REM this is a remark
```

If you press the Ins key and then the Tab key, blanks are inserted up to position 17:

```
10 REM th        is is a remark
```

Correcting the Current Line

Since any line of text typed while BASIC is at the command level is processed by the Program Editor, you can use any of the keys described in the previous section to make corrections on the current line. (BASIC is at the command level after the prompt **Ok** and until you type a RUN command.)

You can extend a logical line over more than one physical screen line by simply typing beyond the edge of the screen. The cursor will *wrap* to the next screen line.

You can also use a line feed (Ctrl-Enter) to print subsequent text on the next screen line. The logical line is not processed until you press Enter.

The line feed actually fills the remainder of the physical screen line with blank characters. These blanks are included in the 255 characters allowed for a BASIC line. (A line feed character is not added to the text and is not counted in the line.)

When the Enter key is finally pressed, the entire logical line is passed to BASIC for processing.

Changing Characters: If you are typing a line and discover you typed something incorrectly, you can correct it. Use the Cursor Left or other cursor movement keys (explained in the previous section) to move the cursor to the position where the mistake occurred, and type the correct letters on top of the wrong ones. Then, move the cursor back to the end of the line using the Cursor Right or End keys, and continue typing.

Erasing Characters: If you notice you've typed an extra character in the line you're typing, you can erase (delete) it using the Del key. Use the Cursor Left or other cursor movement keys to move the cursor to the character you want to erase. Press the Del key, and the

unwanted character is deleted. Then use the Cursor
Right or End keys to move the cursor back to the end
of the line, and continue typing.

Adding Characters: If you see that you've omitted
characters in the line you're typing, move the cursor to
the position where you want to put the new characters.
Press the Ins key to get into Insert Mode. Type the
characters you want to add. The characters you type
will be inserted at the cursor. The characters above and
following it will be pushed to the right. As before,
when you're ready to continue typing at the end of the
line, use the Cursor Right or End keys to move the
cursor there and just continue typing. Insert Mode will
automatically be turned off when you use either of
these keys.

Erasing Part of a Line: To erase to the end of a line
on the screen, press Ctrl-End.

For example, suppose you have typed the following:

```
10 REM *** this is a remark
```

You decide you would like to change the line. You
have the cursor positioned under the **t** in the first word
this, so all you have to do to erase the rest of the line is
press Ctrl-End:

```
10 REM ***  _
```

Canceling a Line: To cancel a line that is being typed,
press the Esc key anywhere in the line. You do not
have to press Enter. The entire line beginning with the
previous Enter will be erased.

For example, suppose you have this line:

```
THIS IS A LINE THAT HAS NO MEANING_
```

Even though the cursor is at the end of the line, the
entire line is erased when you press Esc:

```
_
```

Entering or Changing a BASIC Program

A BASIC program line always begins with a line number, ends with an Enter, and can contain a maximum of 255 characters, including the Enter. If a line contains more than 255 characters, the extra characters are truncated (removed) when Enter is pressed. Even though the extra characters still appear on the screen, they are not processed by BASIC.

You can enter BASIC keywords and variable names in any combination of uppercase (capital) and lowercase (small) letters. The Program Editor will convert everything to uppercase except remarks, DATA statements, and strings enclosed in quotation marks.

BASIC will sometimes change in other ways something you have entered. For example, suppose you use the question mark (?) instead of the word PRINT in a program line. (The ? is a shorthand way of entering PRINT.) When you later list the line, the ? will be changed to PRINT with a space after it. If this expansion causes the line to exceed the maximum of 255 characters, the excess characters will be cut off.

Editing a Program Line on the Screen

You can edit any program line on the screen. First, move the cursor to the place where the change is to be made. Then you can use any or all of the techniques described in this section to change, delete, or add characters to the line. The changes will not become part of your program until you press Enter.

If you want to modify program lines that are not displayed at the moment, you can use the EDIT or LIST command to display them. See "EDIT Command" and "LIST Command" in the *BASIC Reference*.

You can duplicate a line in a program by moving the cursor to the line to be duplicated and then changing the line number to the new line number by typing over the numbers. When you press Enter, both the old line and the new line are in the program.

Note that when you are making corrections to a line you have already entered, you do not have to move the cursor to the end of that logical line before pressing Enter. The Program Editor knows where each logical line ends and it processes the whole line even if the Enter is pressed at the beginning of the line.

> **Note:** Use of the AUTO command can be very helpful when you are entering your program. However, you should exit AUTO mode by pressing Ctrl-Break before changing any lines other than the current one.

Remember, changes made using these techniques change only the program in memory. To permanently save the program with the new changes, use the SAVE command before entering a NEW command or leaving BASIC. See "SAVE Command" in the *BASIC Reference*.

Adding a New Line to a Program: Type a valid line number (Ø through 65529) that has not already been used in the program, then at least one nonblank character, then Enter. The line is saved as part of the BASIC program in storage.

If a line already exists that has the same line number as the line you have just entered, the old line is erased and replaced with the new one.

If you try to add a line to a program when there is no more room in storage, an **Out of memory** error occurs and the line is not added.

Replacing a Program Line: You can replace an existing line by typing the number of the line already in the program, the new text as you want it to appear, and then Enter.

Deleting a Program Line: To delete an existing program line, type only the number of the line and then press Enter. For example, if you enter:

```
10
```

line 1Ø is deleted from the program.

To delete a group of program lines, use the DELETE command. See "DELETE Command" in the *BASIC Reference.*

Do not use the Esc key to delete program lines. Esc causes a line to be erased only from the screen, not from the BASIC program.

> **Note:** If you try to delete a nonexistent line, an **Undefined line number** error occurs.

Deleting an Entire Program: To delete the entire program that currently resides in memory, enter the NEW command. See "NEW Command" in the *BASIC Reference.*

Syntax Errors

When a syntax error is encountered during the running of a program, BASIC displays a **Syntax error** message along with the number of the line that contains the error. Then the line itself is displayed so you can correct it. For example:

```
10 A = 2$12
RUN
Syntax error in 10
10 A = 2$12
```

Notice that BASIC has positioned the cursor at the beginning of the line, under the digit 1. To correct the error, move the cursor right to the dollar sign ($), change it to a plus sign (+), and then press Enter. The corrected line is now stored back in the program.

When you edit a line and store it back in the program while the program is interrupted (as in this example), certain things happen, primarily:

- All variables and arrays are lost. That is, they are reset to zero or null.

- Any files that were open are closed.

- You cannot use CONT to continue the program.

Running a BASIC Program

Two steps are involved in using a BASIC program that you have on a diskette.

The first step is getting a copy of the program transferred from the diskette into the computer's memory. This is called *loading* the program and is done with the LOAD command.

The second step is the actual performance of the program's instructions. This is called *running* the program and is done with the RUN command. RUN *filespec* loads and runs the program specified.

Let's go through the sequence, using the SAMPLES program on the DOS Supplemental Programs diskette.

SAMPLES Program

1. Make sure DOS is ready and **A>** is displayed.

2. Insert the DOS diskette into drive A if it is not already there.

3. Type:

```
basic
```

and press Enter.

This loads Disk BASIC into the computer's memory. You'll see the BASIC prompt (**Ok**), the IBM BASIC copyright, and, across the bottom of the screen, the ten BASIC function keys.

4. Remove the DOS diskette and insert the DOS Supplemental Programs diskette in drive A.

5. Type:

```
run "samples
```

and press Enter.

6. When the SAMPLES title screen is displayed, press the space bar. You will see the *menu* screen.

7. Select the item you want from the menu screen. Note the remarks next to the menu items. They tell you what you need to run the program you selected: whether you need to use Advanced BASIC (BASICA), whether you need a Color/Graphics Monitor, and the amount of memory you need in your system to run these sample programs.

Notice that Advanced BASIC is required for some of the sample programs, but you can use Advanced BASIC to run any of them.

Try program H, COLORBAR. Type:

```
h
```

You do not have to press Enter. If you have a monochrome monitor, you will see two rows of bars in one color. If you have a color monitor, you will see bars of various colors. Adjust the monitor controls as necessary until you achieve a pleasing and appropriate display.

After you have entered your program selection, follow the instructions on the screen. Press Esc to stop a program and return to the menu.

When you have tried the programs you want to see and have returned to the menu, press Esc again. You will see the BASIC prompt, **Ok**.

COMM Program

A sample telecommunications program is included on the DOS Supplemental Programs diskette. This program lets you establish an asynchronous communications link with another IBM Personal Computer, an IBM Series/1 computer, or two communications network services.

To use the COMM program, you need the optional Asynchronous Communications Adapter, equipment, and subscriptions. If you need help, consult your place of purchase.

> **Note:** The COMM program can serve as a model for writing your own telecommunications program.

If you have an Asynchronous Communications Adapter, you can look at the COMM program menu, even if you don't plan to communicate with another computer.

Running a BASIC Program From Another Diskette

You can run a BASIC program from any diskette by loading BASIC first and then specifying the drive and/or path where your program is located.

With One Diskette Drive

With a one-drive system you do not need to change or add a drive specification to *filespec*. Simply insert the diskette into the drive after you have invoked BASIC.

1. Load BASIC.

2. Remove the DOS diskette from drive A and insert into drive A the diskette that contains your program.

3. Load and run your program.

With More Than One Diskette Drive

With a system with more than one drive you need to specify the location of your program.

1. Load BASIC.

2. Load and run your program from the drive or path you specified.

Chapter 3. General Information about Programming in BASIC

Contents

Line Format

Program lines in a BASIC program have the following format:

```
nnnnn BASIC statement[:BASIC statement...]['comment]
```

and they end with Enter.

Line Numbers: "nnnnn" is a line number one to five digits long. Line numbers show the order in which the program lines are stored and serve as reference points for branching and editing. Line numbers must be in the range Ø to 65529. A period (.) can be used in LIST, AUTO, DELETE, and EDIT commands to refer to the current line.

BASIC Statements: A BASIC statement is either *executable* or *nonexecutable*. Executable statements are instructions that tell BASIC what to do next while running a program. For example, **PRINT X** is an executable statement. Nonexecutable statements, such as DATA or REM, contain information only and do not cause any program action when BASIC sees them. All the BASIC statements are explained in detail in the *BASIC Reference*.

You can, if you wish, have more than one BASIC statement on a line, but each statement must be separated from the one before it by a colon. The total number of characters cannot exceed 255, including the Enter. For example:

```
10 FOR I=1 TO 5: PRINT I: NEXT
RUN
 1
 2
 3
 4
 5
```

Comments: Comments can be included at the end of a line. The ' (single quote) separates the comment from the rest of the line.

Character Set

The BASIC character set consists of alphabetic characters (A-Z), numeric characters (Ø-9), and special characters.

The following special characters have specific meanings in BASIC:

Character	Name
	blank
=	equal sign or assignment symbol
+	plus sign or concatenation symbol
-	minus sign
*	asterisk or multiplication symbol
/	slash or division symbol
\	backslash; integer division symbol or path delimiter
^	caret or exponentiation symbol
(	left parenthesis
)	right parenthesis
%	percent sign or integer type-declaration character
#	number (or pound) sign, or double-precision type declaration character
$	dollar sign or string type-declaration character
!	exclamation point or single-precision type-declaration character
&	ampersand
,	comma
.	period or decimal point
'	single quotation mark (apostrophe), or remark delimiter
;	semicolon
:	colon or statement separator
?	question mark (PRINT abbreviation)
<	less than
>	greater than
"	double quotation mark or string delimiter
_	underline

Many characters can be printed or displayed even though they have no particular meaning to BASIC. See Appendix D, "ASCII Character Codes," in the *BASIC Reference* for a complete list of these characters.

Reserved Words

Certain words and letter combinations have special meaning to BASIC. They are called *reserved words*. Reserved words include all BASIC commands, statements, function names, and operator names. Reserved words cannot be used as variable names.

Reserved words must be separated from data or other parts of a BASIC statement by blanks or special characters as allowed by the syntax.

The following are reserved words in BASIC.

ABS	DATE$
AND	DEF
ASC	DEFDBL
ATN	DEFINT
AUTO	DEFSNG
BEEP	DEFSTR
BLOAD	DELETE
BSAVE	DIM
CALL	DRAW
CDBL	EDIT
CHAIN	ELSE
CHDIR	END
CHR$	ENVIRON
CINT	ENVIRON$
CIRCLE	EOF
CLEAR	EQV
CLOSE	ERASE
CLS	ERDEV
COLOR	ERDEV$
COM	ERL
COMMON	ERR
CONT	ERROR
COS	EXP
CSNG	FIELD
CSRLIN	FILES
CVD	FIX
CVI	FN*xxxxxxxx*
CVS	
DATA	

FOR	NEW
FRE	NEXT
GET	NOT
GOSUB	OCT$
GOTO	OFF
HEX$	ON
IF	OPEN
IMP	OPTION
INKEY$	OR
INP	OUT
INPUT	PAINT
INPUT#	PEEK
INPUT$	PEN
INSTR	PLAY
INT	PMAP
INTER$	POINT
IOCTL	POKE
IOCTL$	POS
KEY	PRESET
KILL	PRINT
LEFT$	PRINT#
LEN	PSET
LET	PUT
LINE	RANDOMIZE
LIST	READ
LLIST	REM
LOAD	RENUM
LOC	RESET
LOCATE	RESTORE
LOF	RESUME
LOG	RETURN
LPOS	RIGHT$
LPRINT	RMDIR
LSET	RND
MERGE	RSET
MID$	RUN
MKDIR	SAVE
MKD$	SCREEN
MKI$	SGN
MKS$	SHELL
MOD	SIN
MOTOR	SOUND
NAME	SPACE$

SPC(	TRON
SQR	USING
STEP	USR
STICK	VAL
STOP	VARPTR
STR$	VARPTR$
STRIG	VIEW
STRING$	WAIT
SWAP	WEND
SYSTEM	WHILE
TAB(	WIDTH
TAN	WINDOW
THEN	WRITE
TIME$	WRITE#
TIMER	XOR
TO	
TROFF	

Constants

Constants are values that you supply when you write a
BASIC program and that do not change during program
execution. There are two types of constants: string
(character) constants and numeric constants.

A string constant is a sequence of up to 255 characters
enclosed in double quotation marks. The characters can
be letters, numbers, or symbols. Examples of string
constants:

```
"HELLO"
"$25,000.00"
"Number of Employees"
```

There are a few cases where BASIC knows that a
particular thing must be a string constant, and the
quotation marks are not required. These cases are
noted where appropriate in this book. Also, if you start
a string with a quotation mark, but forget to add the
end quotation mark, BASIC assumes that a quotation

mark is at the end of the line. However, this produces correct results only when the string is the last thing on the line.

Numeric constants are positive or negative numbers. A plus sign (+) is optional on a positive number. Negative numbers must be signed. Numeric constants in BASIC cannot contain commas. There are five ways to indicate numeric constants:

Integer
Whole numbers between -32768 and +32767, inclusive. Integer constants do not have decimal points.

Fixed point
Positive or negative real numbers; that is, numbers that contain decimal points.

Floating point
Positive or negative numbers represented in exponential form (similar to scientific notation). In single-precision calculation, a floating point constant consists of an optionally signed integer or fixed point number (the mantissa) followed by the letter E and an optionally signed integer (the exponent). Double-precision floating point constants use the letter D instead of E. The E (or D) means "times ten to the power of."

You can represent any number from 2.9E-39 to 1.7E+38 (positive or negative) as a floating point constant.

For more information, see the next section, "Numeric Precision."

For example:

```
23E-2
```

Here, 23 is the mantissa, and -2 is the exponent. This number could be read as "23 times 1∅ to the negative two power."You could write it as ∅.23 in regular fixed-point notation.

More examples:

```
235.988E-7
```

This is a single-precision number equivalent to .∅∅∅∅235988.

```
2359D6
```

This is a double-precision number equivalent to 2359∅∅∅∅∅.

Remember, when you read floating point notation: E indicates single-precision calculation and D indicates double-precision calculation.

Hex

Hexadecimal integer numbers up to four digits, with a prefix of &H. Hexadecimal digits are the numbers Ø through 9, A, B, C, D, E, and F. Examples:

```
&H76
&H32F
```

Octal

Octal integer numbers up to six digits, with the prefix &O or just &. Octal digits are Ø through 7. Examples:

```
&O347
&1234
```

Numeric Precision

Numbers can be stored internally as integer, single-precision, or double-precision numbers. Constants entered in integer, hex, or octal format are stored in two bytes of memory and are interpreted as integers (whole numbers). With double-precision calculation, the numbers are stored with 17 digits of precision and printed with up to 16 digits. With single-precision calculation, seven digits are stored and up to seven digits are printed, although only six digits may be accurate. Seven digits are printed in single precision because any intermediary processing uses all seven digits. To ensure the accuracy of final results, enter all seven digits *before* the final results when you do interactive processing.

A single-precision constant is any numeric constant written with any one of the following:

- seven or fewer digits

- exponential form using E

- trailing exclamation point (!)

A double-precision constant is any numeric constant written with any one of the following:

- eight or more digits

- exponential form using D

- trailing number sign (#)

The following table summarizes the precision and range of integers, single-precision numbers, and double-precision numbers:

TYPE	RANGE	ACCURACY
Integer	-32768 to 32767	Perfect
Single-precision floating point	1ØE-38 to 1ØE+38	6 decimal digits
Double-precision floating point	1ØD-38 to 1ØD+38	16 decimal digits

Examples of single- and double-precision constants:

Single-Precision	Double-Precision
46.8	345692811
-1.Ø9E-Ø6	-1.Ø9432D-Ø6
3489.Ø	3489.Ø#
22.5!	7654321.1234

How BASIC Converts Numbers from One Precision to Another

When necessary, BASIC converts a number from one precision to another according to the following rules:

1. If a numeric value of one precision is assigned to a numeric variable of a different precision, the number is stored as the precision declared in the target variable name.

   Example:

   ```
   10 A% = 23.42
   20 PRINT A%
   RUN
    23
   ```

2. Rounding up, as opposed to truncation, occurs when assigning any higher precision value to a lower precision variable (for example, changing from double- to single-precision values).

   Example:

   ```
   10 C = 55.8834567#
   20 PRINT C
   RUN
    55.88346
   ```

   This affects not only assignment statements (e.g., I%=2.5 results in I%=3), but also function and statement evaluations. For instance, TAB(4.5) goes to the fifth position; A(1.5) is the same as A(2); and X=11.5 MOD 4 results in a value of 0 for X.

3. If you convert from a lower precision to a higher precision number, the resulting higher precision number cannot be any more accurate than the lower precision number. For example, if you assign a single-precision value (A) to a double-precision variable (B#), only the first six digits of B# will be accurate because only six digits of accuracy were supplied with A. The error can be bounded using the following formula:

```
ABS(B#-A) < 6.3E-8 * A
```

That is, the absolute value of the difference between the printed double-precision number and the original single-precision value is less than 6.3E-8 times the original single-precision value.

Example:

```
10 A = 2.04
20 B# = A
30 PRINT A;B#
RUN
 2.04 2.039999961853027
```

4. When an expression is evaluated, all the operands in an arithmetic or relational operation are converted to the same degree of precision, namely the most precise operand. Also, the result of an arithmetic operation is returned to this degree of precision.

Examples:

```
10 D# = 6#/7
20 PRINT D#
RUN
 .8571428571428571
```

The arithmetic is performed in double precision and the result is returned in D# as a double-precision value.

```
10 D = 6#/7
20 PRINT D
RUN
 .8571429
```

The arithmetic is performed in double precision and the result is returned to D (single-precision variable), rounded, and printed as a single-precision value.

5. Logical operators (see "Logical Operators" in this chapter) convert their operands to integers and return an integer result. Operands must be in the range -32768 to 32767 or an **Overflow** error occurs.

Variables

Variables are names used to represent values in a BASIC program. As with constants, there are two types of variables: numeric and string. A numeric variable always has a number value. A string variable can only have a character string value. A string variable can have up to 255 characters.

You can give a variable an unchanging value (such as *salary* equals a certain amount) or you can set its value to be the result of calculations or data input statements in the program (such as *salary* equals 1∅% of sales). In any case, the variable type (string or numeric) must match the type of data assigned to it.

If you use a numeric variable before you assign a value to it, its value is assumed to be zero. String variables are initially assumed to be null; that is, they have no characters in them and have a length of zero.

How to Name a Variable

BASIC allows a variable name to be up to 4∅ characters in length.

The characters can be letters, numbers, and decimal points. The first character must be a letter. Special characters that identify the type of variable are also allowed as the last character of the name. For more information about types, see the next section, "How to Declare Variable Types."

A variable name cannot be a reserved word, but it can contain imbedded reserved words. (See "Reserved Words," earlier in this chapter, for a complete list of reserved words.) For example:

```
10 EXP = 5
```

is invalid, because EXP is a reserved word. However,

```
10 EXPONENT = 5
```

is okay, because EXP is imbedded in the variable name.

> **Note:** A variable beginning with FN is assumed to
> be a call to a user-defined function. See "DEF FN
> Statement" in the *BASIC Reference.*

How to Declare Variable Types

A variable name determines its type (string or numeric,
and if numeric, its precision).

String variable names are written with a dollar sign ($)
as the last character. For example:

```
A$ = "SALES REPORT"
```

The dollar sign is a variable type-declaration character.
It "declares" that the variable will represent a string.

Numeric variable names can declare integer, single-, or
double-precision values. Although computations with
single-precision variables are less accurate, there are
advantages to using them:

- They require less storage.

- They can be calculated faster.

The type-declaration characters for numeric variables
and the number of bytes required to store each type of
value are:

%   Integer variable (2 bytes)

!   Single-precision variable (4 bytes)

Double-precision variable (8 bytes)

> **Note:** If the type-declaration character is not
> specified, the default is single precision.

Examples of variable names with type-declaration characters are:

```
PI#        declares a double-precision value
MINIMUM!   declares a single-precision value
LIMIT%     declares an integer value
N$         declares a string value
ABC        defaults to a single-precision value
```

Variable types can also be declared in another way. The BASIC statements DEFINT, DEFSNG, DEFDBL, and DEFSTR can be included in a program to declare the types for certain variable names. These statements are described under "DEFtype Statements" in the *BASIC Reference*. All the examples in this book assume that no DEFtype statements were used (unless they are explicitly shown in the examples).

Arrays

An *array* is a list or table of values that is referred to by a single name. Each value in the array is called an *element*. Elements are string or numeric variables and can be used in expressions and in BASIC statements.

The *subscript* (the number in parentheses) indicates the position of an element in an array. Zero is the first position unless you explicity change it. See "OPTION BASE Statement" in the *BASIC Reference*.

Declaring the name and type of an array and setting the number of elements and their arrangement within it is known as *defining*, or *dimensioning*, the array. The maximum number of dimensions for an array is 255.

If you use an array element before you define (dimension) the array, it is assumed to be dimensioned with a maximum subscript of 1$\emptyset$. That is, only the first eleven elements (indexed $\emptyset$ to 1$\emptyset$) will be recognized.

To define an array, use the DIM statement.

For example:

`DIM B$(5)`

This statement creates a one-dimensional, string-variable array named B$ with a maximum of 6 elements. Array B$ can be thought of as a list of character strings:

B$(0)
B$(1)
B$(2)
B$(3)
B$(4)
B$(5)

Another example:

`DIM A(2,3)`

This statement creates a two-dimensional, numeric-variable array named A. Since the array does not include a type-declaration character, the array by default consists of single-precision values.

Array A can be thought of as a table of rows and columns:

A(0,0)	A(∅,1)	A(∅,2)	A(∅,3)
A(1,∅)	A(1,1)	A(1,2)	A(1,3)
A(2,∅)	A(2,1)	A(2,2)	A(2,3)

The element in the second row, first column, is called A(1,∅).

Here is a sample program:

```
10 DIM YEARS(3,4)
20 YEARS(2,3)=84
30 FOR ROW=0 TO 3
40 FOR COLUMN=0 TO 4
50 PRINT YEARS(ROW,COLUMN);
60 NEXT COLUMN
70 PRINT
80 NEXT ROW
RUN
 0 0 0 0 0
 0 0 0 0 0
 0 0 0 840
 0 0 0 0 0
```

In this program, line 1∅ dimensions an array with 2∅ elements (4 rows and 5 columns). Line 2∅ assigns the array element at position 2,3 the value of 84. The nested loops in lines 3∅-8∅ print the array as a 4 by 5 matrix.

Note: A scalar variable can have the same name as an array variable because A$ is different from any element in array A$ (n,...).

Techniques for Formatting Your Output

BASIC has built-in statements and functions that you can use in your programs to display numbers in the desired format and with the desired accuracy.

- Use DEFDBL to define your constants and variables as double-precision numbers to format your output. For example:

```
10 WIDTH 80
20 DEFDBL A
30 A=70#
40 PRINT A/100#,
50 A=A+1
60 IF A<100# GOTO 40

RUN
```

.7	.71	.72	.73	.74
.75	.76	.77	.78	.79
.8	.81	.82	.83	.84
.85	.86	.87	.88	.89
.9	.91	.92	.93	.94
.95	.96	.97	.98	.99

- To display program results in decimal notation, use the PRINT USING and LPRINT USING statements. These statements let you choose the format in which the results will be printed or displayed.

```
10 FOR I=4 to 5 STEP .1
20 PRINT USING "#.#   ";I;
30 NEXT

RUN

4.0 4.1 4.2 4.3 4.4 4.5 4.6 4.7 4.8 4.9 5.0
```

Notes:

1. Avoid using both single- and double-precision numbers in the same formula because it reduces accuracy.

2. Use double-precision transcendental functions for greater accuracy.

Numeric Expressions and Operators

A numeric expression can be simply a numeric constant or variable. It can also be an operator, combining constants and variables to produce a single numeric value.

Numeric operators perform mathematical or logical operations, most often on numeric values, but sometimes on string values. They are called numeric operators because they produce a value that is a number. BASIC numeric operators can be divided into the following categories:

- Arithmetic
- Relational
- Logical
- Functions

Arithmetic Operators

The arithmetic operators perform the usual arithmetic operations in the standard mathematical order of preference; that is, when an expression contains more than one operation, they will be carried out in the following order:

Operator	Operation	Sample Expression
∧	Exponentiation	X∧Y
-	Negation	-X
*, /	Multiplication, Floating Point Division	X*Y X/Y
\	Integer Division	X\Y
MOD	Modulo Arithmetic	X MOD Y
+, -	Addition, Subtraction	X+Y X-Y

Although most of these operations probably look familiar to you, two of them - integer division and modulo arithmetic - may need some explanation.

Integer Division: Integer division is denoted by a backslash (\). The operands are rounded to integers (in the range -32768 through 32767) before the division is performed; the quotient is truncated to an integer.

For example:

```
1Ø A = 1Ø\4
2Ø B = 25.68\6.99
3Ø PRINT A;B
RUN
 2  3
```

Modulo Arithmetic: Modulo arithmetic is denoted by the operator MOD. It gives the integer value that is the remainder of an integer division.

For example:

```
1Ø A = 7 MOD 4
2Ø PRINT A
RUN
 3
```

This result occurs because 7/4 is 1, with remainder 3.

```
PRINT 25.68 MOD 6.99
 5
```

The result is 5 because 26/7 is 3, with the remainder 5. (Remember, BASIC rounds when converting to integers.)

Relational Operators

Relational operators compare two values. The values can both be either numeric or string. The result of the comparison is either "true" (-1) or "false" (Ø). This result is usually used to make a decision regarding program flow. See "IF Statement" in the *BASIC Reference.*

Operator	Relation Tested	Sample Expression
=	Equality	X=Y
<> or ><	Inequality	X<>Y X><Y
<	Less than	X<Y
>	Greater than	X>Y
<= or =<	Less than or equal to	X<=Y X=<Y
>= or =>	Greater than or equal to	X>=Y X=>Y

(The equal sign is also used to assign a value to a variable. See "LET Statement" in the *BASIC Reference*.)

Numeric Comparisons: When arithmetic and relational operators are combined in one expression, the arithmetic is always performed first. For example, the expression:

```
X+Y < (T-1)/Z
```

is true (-1) if the value of X plus Y is less than the value of T-1 divided by Z.

String Comparisons: String comparisons can be thought of as "alphabetical." That is, a string is "less than" another if the first letter of it comes before the other one alphabetically. Lowercase letters are "greater than" their uppercase counterparts. Numbers are "less than" letters.

The way two strings are actually compared is by taking one character at a time from each string and comparing the ASCII codes. See Appendix D, "ASCII Character Codes," in the *BASIC Reference*. If all the ASCII codes are the same, the strings are equal. Otherwise, as soon as the ASCII codes differ, the string with the lower code number is less than the string with the higher code number. If, during string comparison, the end of one string is reached, the shorter string is said to be smaller. Leading and trailing blanks are significant. For example, all the following relational expressions are true (that is, the result of the relational operation is -1):

```
"AA" < "AB"
"FILENAME" = "FILENAME"
"X&" > "X#"
"kg" > "KG"
"RICH" < "RICHB"
B$ < "718"   (where B$ = "12543")
```

All string constants used in comparison expressions must be enclosed in quotation marks.

Logical Operators

Logical operators perform logical, or *boolean*, operations on numeric values. Just as the relational operators are usually used to make decisions regarding program flow, logical operators are usually used to connect two or more relations and return a true or false value to be used in a decision. See "IF Statement" in the *BASIC Reference*.

A logical operator takes a combination of true-false values and returns a true or false result. An operand of a logical operator is considered to be true if it is not equal to zero (like the -1 returned by a relational operator); or false if it is equal to zero. The number is calculated by performing the operation bit by bit.

The logical operators are: NOT (logical complement), AND (conjunction), OR (disjunction), XOR (exclusive or), IMP (implication), and EQV (equivalence). Each operator returns results as indicated in the following table. (T indicates a true, or nonzero value. F indicates a false, or zero value.) The operators are listed in order of precedence.

NOT

X	NOT X
T	F
F	T

AND

X	Y	X AND Y
T	T	T
T	F	F
F	T	F
F	F	F

OR

X	Y	X OR Y
T	T	T
T	F	T
F	T	T
F	F	F

XOR

X	Y	X XOR Y
T	T	F
T	F	T
F	T	T
F	F	F

EQV

X	Y	X EQV Y
T	T	T
T	F	F
F	T	F
F	F	T

IMP

X	Y	X IMP Y
T	T	T
T	F	F
F	T	T
F	F	T

Some examples of ways to use logical operators in decisions:

```
IF HE>60 AND SHE<20 THEN 1000
```

Here, the result is true if the value of the variable HE is more than 6Ø and the value of SHE is less than 2Ø.

```
50 IF NOT (P=-1) THEN 100
```

Here, the program branches to line 1ØØ if P is not equal to -1. Note that NOT (P=-1) does not produce the same result as NOT P. See the next section, "How Logical Operators Work," for an explanation.

```
100 FLAG% = NOT FLAG%
```

This example switches a value back and forth from true to false.

How Logical Operators Work: Operands are converted to integers in the range -32768 to +32767. (If the operands are not in this range, an **Overflow** error results.) If the operand is negative, the twos complement form is used. This turns each operand into a sequence of 16 bits. The operation is performed on these sequences. That is, each bit of the result is determined by the corresponding bits in the two operands, according to the tables for the operator listed previously. A 1 bit is considered "true" and a Ø bit is "false".

Thus, you can use logical operators to test for a particular bit pattern. For instance, the AND operator may be used to "mask" all but one of the bits of a status byte at a machine I/O port.

The following examples show how the logical operators work.

```
A = 63 AND 16
```

Here, A is set to 16. Since 63 is binary 111111 and 16 is binary 1ØØØØ, 63 AND 16 equals Ø1ØØØØ in binary, which is equal to 16.

```
B = -1 AND 8
```

B is set to 8. Since -1 is binary 11111111 11111111 and 8 is binary 1ØØØ, -1 AND 8 equals binaryØØØØØØØØØØØØ1ØØØ, or 8.

```
C = 4 OR 2
```

Here, C equals 6. Since 4 is binary 1ØØ and 2 is binary Ø1Ø, 4 OR 2 is binary 11Ø, which is equal to 6.

```
X = 2
TWOSCOMP = (NOT X) + 1
```

This example shows how to form the twos complement of a number. X is 2, which is 1Ø binary. NOT X is then binary 11111111 111111Ø1, which is -3 in decimal; -3 plus 1 is -2, the complement of 2. That is, the twos complement of any integer is the bit complement plus one.

Note that if both operands are equal to eitherØ or -1, a logical operator returns either Ø or -1.

Numeric Functions

A function is used like a variable in an expression to call a predetermined operation that is to be performed on one or more operands. BASIC has some built-in numeric functions that reside in the system, such as SQR (square root) and SIN (sine).

You can also define your own numeric functions using the DEF FN statement. See "DEF FN Statement" in the *BASIC Reference*.

Order of Execution

In the previous sections, the categories of numeric operations have been discussed in their order of precedence, and the precedence of each operation within a category was indicated in the discussion of the category. In summary:

1. Function calls are evaluated first.

2. Arithmetic operations are performed next, in this order:

   a. ^
   b. unary -
   c. *, /
   d. \
   e. MOD
   f. +, -

3. Relational operations are done next.

4. Logical operations are done last, in this order:

   a. NOT
   b. AND
   c. OR
   d. XOR
   e. EQV
   f. IMP

Operations at the same level in the list are performed in left-to-right order. To change the order in which the operations are performed, use parentheses. Operations within parentheses are performed first. Inside parentheses, the usual order of operations is maintained.

Here are some sample algebraic expressions and their BASIC counterparts.

Algebraic Expression	BASIC Expression
$X+2Y$	$X+Y*2$
$X-\dfrac{Y}{Z}$	$X-Y/Z$
$\dfrac{XY}{Z}$	$X*Y/Z$
$\dfrac{X+Y}{Z}$	$(X+Y)/Z$
$(X^2)^Y$	$(X\char`^2)\char`^Y$
X^{Y^Z}	$X\char`^(Y\char`^Z)$
$X(-Y)$	$X*(-Y)$

Note: Two consecutive operators must be separated by parentheses, as shown in the **X*(-Y)** example.

String Expressions and Operators

A string expression can be simply a string constant or variable, or it can combine constants and variables by using operators to produce a single string value.

String operators are used to arrange character strings in different ways. The two categories of string operators are:

- Concatenation
- Function

Note that although you can use the relational operators =, <>, <, >, <=, and >= to compare two strings, these are not considered to be "string operators" because they produce a numeric result, not a string result. Read through "Relational Operators" earlier in this chapter for an explanation of how you can compare strings using relational operators.

Concatenation

Joining two strings together is called *concatenation*. Strings are concatenated using the plus symbol (+). For example:

```
10 COMPANY$ = "IBM"
20 TYPE$ = " Personal"
30 FULLNAME$ = TYPE$ + " Computer"
40 PRINT COMPANY$+FULLNAME$
RUN
IBM Personal Computer
```

String Functions

A string function is like a numeric function except that it returns a string result. A string function can be used in an expression to call a predetermined operation that is to be performed on one or more operands. BASIC has built-in string functions that reside in the system, such as MID$, which returns a string from the middle of another string, and CHR$, which returns the character with the specified ASCII code.

You can also define your own string functions using the DEF FN statement. See "DEF FN Statement" in the *BASIC Reference*.

Input and Output

The remainder of this chapter contains information on input and output (I/O) in BASIC. The following topics are discussed: naming and using files and paths; using I/O devices;tree structured directories; device support; and displaying output on the screen in text and graphics modes.

Files

A *file* is a collection of information that is kept somewhere other than in the random access memory of the IBM Personal Computer; for example, on disk or cassette. To access the information, you must open the file with the OPEN statement. Then you can use the file for input and/or output.

BASIC supports the concept of general device I/O files. This means that any type of input/output can be treated like I/O to a file, whether you are actually using a cassette or disk file, or you are using your computer to communicate with another computer.

File Number

BASIC performs I/O operations using a file number. You assign the number to a file or device when you open it with the OPEN statement. See "OPEN Statement" in the *BASIC Reference*.

A file number can be any number, variable, or expression ranging from 1 to the maximum number of files that can be open at the same time. See /F switch in "Options in the BASIC Command Line" in Chapter 2.

Filename

The filename must conform to the following rules:

For cassette files:

- The name cannot be more than eight characters.

- The name cannot contain colons, hexØØs, or hex FFs (decimal 255s).

For disk files, the name must conform to DOS conventions:

- The name can consist of two parts separated by a period (.):

  name.extension

  The *name* can be from one to eight characters. The *extension* can be from one to three characters.

  If more than three characters are entered for *extension*, the extra characters are truncated. If *name* is longer than eight characters and *extension* is not included, BASIC inserts a period after the eighth character and uses the extra characters (up to three) for the *extension*. If *name* is longer than eight characters and an *extension* is included, an error occurs.

- Only the following characters are allowed in *name* and *extension*:

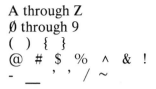

A through Z
∅ through 9
( ) { }
@ # $ % ^ & !
- _ ' ' / ~

Note: Previous releases of BASIC allowed the characters <, >, and \ to be used within a filename, but these characters have special meaning to BASIC 2.∅ and later releases and can no longer be used in filenames.

Some examples of filenames for Disk BASIC and Advanced BASIC are:

27HAL.DAD
VDL
PROGRAM1.BAS
$$@(!).123

The following examples show how BASIC shortens
names and extensions when they are too long.

A23456789JKLMN becomes: A2345678.9JK
@HOME.TRUM1∅ becomes: @HOME.TRU
SHERRYLYNN.BAS causes an error

Device Name

The device name consists of up to four alphanumeric
characters followed by a colon (:). It is a name
assigned to input/output devices for the IBM Personal
Computer. Device names and what they apply to are as
follows:

KYBD: Keyboard. Input only. All versions of BASIC.
SCRN: Screen. Output only. All versions of BASIC.
LPT1: First printer. Output, all versions; or random
access, Disk BASIC and Advanced BASIC.
LPT2: Second printer. Output or random access.
Disk BASIC and Advanced BASIC.
LPT3: Third printer. Output or random access. Disk
BASIC and Advanced BASIC.

COMMUNICATIONS DEVICES

COM1: First Asynchronous Communications Adapter. Input and output. Disk BASIC and Advanced BASIC.

COM2: Second Asynchronous Communications Adapter. Input and output. Disk BASIC and Advanced BASIC.

STORAGE DEVICES

CAS1: Cassette tape player. Input and output. All versions.

A: First diskette drive. Input and output. Disk BASIC and Advanced BASIC.

B: Second diskette drive. Input and output. Disk BASIC and Advanced BASIC.

C: First fixed disk drive. Input and output. Disk BASIC and Advanced BASIC.

D:: Second fixed disk drive. Input and output. Disk BASIC and Advanced BASIC.

Note: If you have three diskette drives, the third diskette drive is C:, the first fixed disk is D:, and the second fixed disk is E:. Similarly, if you have four diskette drives, the fourth diskette drive is D:, the first fixed disk is E:, and the second fixed disk is F:.

Naming Files

The file is described by its *file specification*, or *filespec* for short. The file specification is a string expression in the form:

```
[device][path]filename
```

The device name tells BASIC which I/O device is being used. The path tells BASIC which directory contains the file. and the filename tells BASIC *which* file to look

for on that particular device. Sometimes you do not
need both device name and path, so specification of
device and *path* is optional.

All device names end with a colon (:). The colon is
part of the device name and you *must* include it
whenever that device is specified.

> **Note:** File specifications for communications
> devices are different. The filename is replaced with
> a list of options specifying such things as line speed.
> See "OPEN "COM ... Statement" in the *BASIC
> Reference* for details.

If you use a string constant for the *filespec*, you must
enclose it in quotation marks. For example,

```
LOAD "B:PROG.BAS"
```

In Disk BASIC and Advanced BASIC 2.∅ and later
releases, you can specify a *path* to a file in your filespec.

A path is a list of directory names separated by
backslashes (\ ).

You can use paths for the following commands:

BLOAD	KILL	OPEN
BSAVE	LOAD	RMDIR
CHAIN	MERGE	RUN
CHDIR	MKDIR	SAVE
FILES	NAME	

Notes:

1. A path cannot contain more than 63 characters.

2. If you specify a device, place the device name before the path. If you place it anywhere else, you will see a **Bad filename** error message.

3. If you use a string constant for the path, you must enclose it in quotation marks. For example:

   "B:\SALES\JUNE\REPORT\"

If you specify a file that is not in the current directory, you must supply BASIC with a path of directory names so it can locate the file.

Types of Directories

A single directory is created on each disk or diskette when you use the DOS FORMAT command. That directory is called the *root* directory. The maximum number of files in a diskette root directory depends on the media being used. The maximum number of files in a fixed disk root directory depends on the size of the DOS partition on the disk.

In addition to containing the names of files, the root directory also contains the names of other directories called *subdirectories*. Unlike the root directory, these subdirectories are actually files. They can contain any number of additional files and subdirectories—limited only by the amount of available space on the disk.

The subdirectory names are in the same format as filenames. All characters that are valid for filenames are valid for a directory name. Each directory can contain file and directory names that also appear in other directories.

Current Directory

Just as BASIC remembers a default drive, it can also remember a default directory for each drive on your system. This is called the *current directory* and is the directory that BASIC will search if you enter a filename without telling BASIC which directory contains the file. You can change the current directory by issuing the CHDIR command. See "CHDIR Command" in the *BASIC Reference*.

If a filename is included in a path, it must be separated from the previous directory name by a backslash. If a path begins with a backslash, BASIC starts its search from the root directory; otherwise, the search begins at the current directory.

Tree-Structured Directories

Previous releases of BASIC used a simple directory structure for managing files on diskettes. With the added hardware support for fixed disks, a more sophisticated method was needed to manage the thousands of files that a single disk can hold.

BASIC 2.∅ and later releases enable you to better organize and manage your disks by placing groups of related files in their own directories on the same disk or diskette. These directories are known as *tree-structured directories*. These directories begin with the root directory and branch into subdirectories.

For example, if a company has two departments, sales and accounting, that share an IBM Personal Computer, all the company's files can be kept on the computer's fixed disk. The organization of the files might look like this:

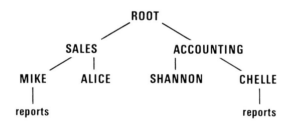

Device Support

BASIC's file I/O system allows the use of user-installed devices. (See the *DOS 3.0 Technical Reference* manual for information on device drivers.)

You could, for instance, write your own device driver to replace LPT1:. Your program would open this driver as follows:

```
OPEN "LPT1" FOR mode AS #filenum
```

Several rules must be followed when writing a device driver.

- The name of the installed device cannot end with a colon. Device names ending with a colon are reserved for certain predefined devices (KEYBD:, SCRN:, etc.).

- LPT1:, LPT2:, and LPT3: are the only system device drivers that can be replaced by an installed device driver having the same name.

- The record length is set to 1 unless changed by the OPEN statement:

```
OPEN filespec [FOR MODE] AS filenum LEN=recl
```

  When this option is used, BASIC will buffer the number of characters equal to *recl* before sending them to the driver.

- BASIC sends only a carriage return (&H0D) at the end of a line. If a line feed (&H0A) is needed, the driver must provide it.

- Your device driver must be able to return an **End of file** condition to BASIC if you want to close a sequential input file open to a device driver. If BASIC attempts to read past the end of the device input stream, the driver should return a ∧Z (Control-Z), which is used by BASIC to produce the **Input past end** error.

Screen Displays

BASIC can display text, special characters, points, lines, and more complex shapes in one color or in full color. How much of this you can do depends on which display adapter you have in your IBM Personal Computer.

Display Adapters

The IBM Monochrome Display and Parallel Printer Adapter, and the Color/Graphics Monitor Adapter are two display adapters available for the IBM Personal Computer.

With the monochrome adapter, text is displayed in one color. *Text* refers to letters, numbers, and all the special characters. You have some capability to draw pictures with the special line and block characters. You can also create blinking, reverse image, invisible, highlighted, and underscored characters by setting parameters in the COLOR statement.

The Color/Graphics Monitor Adapter also operates in text mode, but it allows you to display text in 16 different colors (or one color by setting parameters in the SCREEN or COLOR statements). You also get complete graphics capability to draw complex pictures. This graphics capability makes the screen *all points addressable* in medium and high resolution. This is more versatile than the ability to draw with the special line and block characters that you have in text mode. In this book and in the *BASIC Reference*, the term *graphics* refers only to this special capability of the Color/Graphics Monitor Adapter. The use of the extended character set with special line and block characters is not considered graphics.

Text Mode

The screen can be pictured like this:

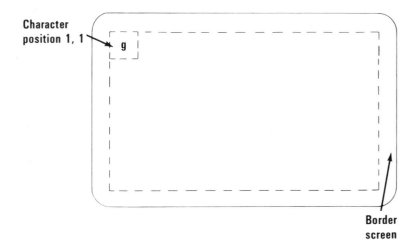

Character position 1, 1

g

Border screen

Characters are shown in 25 horizontal lines across the screen. Line 1 is at the top; line 25 at the bottom. Each line has 4Ø character positions (or 8Ø, depending on how you set the width). These are numbered 1 to 4Ø (or 8Ø) from left to right. The position numbers are used in the LOCATE statement, and are the values returned by the POS(Ø) and CSRLIN functions. For example, the character in the upper left corner of the screen is on line 1, position 1.

Characters are normally placed on the screen through the use of the PRINT statement. Characters are displayed at the position of the cursor from left to right on each line, from line 1 to line 24. When the cursor would normally go to line 25 on the screen, lines 1 through 24 are *scrolled* up one line, so that what was line 1 disappears from the screen. Line 24 is then blank, and the cursor remains on line 24 to continue printing.

Line 25 is usually used for "soft key" display (see "KEY Statement" in the *BASIC Reference*), but you can write over this area of the screen if you turn off the "soft key" display. The 25th line is never scrolled by BASIC.

Each character on the screen is composed of two parts: foreground and background. The foreground is the character itself. The background is the "box" around the character. You can set the foreground and the background color for each character by using the COLOR statement. You can also make characters blink.

You can use a total of 16 different colors if you have the Color/Graphics Monitor Adapter:

Ø Black	8 Gray
1 Blue	9 Light Blue
2 Green	1Ø Light Green
3 Cyan	11 Light Cyan
4 Red	12 Light Red
5 Magenta	13 Light Magenta
6 Brown	14 Yellow
7 White	15 High-intensity White

Colors may vary depending on your display device.

Most television sets or monitors have an area of overscan that is outside the area used for characters. This overscan area is known as the *border screen*. You can use the COLOR statement to set the color of the border screen. Statements you can use to display information in text mode are:

CLS	SCREEN
COLOR	WIDTH
LOCATE	WRITE
PRINT	

The following functions and system variables can be used in text mode:

CSRLIN   SPC
POS   TAB
SCREEN

Another special feature you get in text mode if you have the Color/Graphics Monitor Adapter is multiple display pages. The Color/Graphics Monitor Adapter has a 16K-byte screen buffer, but text mode needs only 2K of that (or 4K for 8Ø-column width). So the buffer is divided into *pages*, which can be written on and/or displayed individually. There are eight pages, numbered Ø to 7, in 4Ø- column width; and four pages, numbered Ø to 3, in 8Ø-column width. See "SCREEN Statement" in the *BASIC Reference*.

Graphics Modes

The graphics modes are available only if you have the Color/Graphics Monitor Adapter.

You can use BASIC statements to draw in two graphic resolutions:

- medium resolution – 32Ø by 2ØØ points and four colors

- high resolution – 64Ø by 2ØØ points and two colors

You can select the resolution you want to use with the SCREEN statement.

The BASIC statements used for graphics are:

CIRCLE   PRESET
COLOR   PSET
DRAW   PUT
GET   SCREEN
LINE   VIEW
PAINT   WINDOW

The graphics functions are:

PMAP
POINT

Color Attributes: There is a numerical value that
describes the color of each point on the screen. This
numerical value is called an attribute. For example, if
you refer to the list of available colors in "COLOR
Statement (Text Mode)" in the *BASIC Reference*, you
will see that the color blue is indexed by the attribute 1.

The attribute varies depending on the current screen
mode. The variance is based on the attribute range for
each mode. The maximum attribute for each mode
determines how many bits are required to define the
attribute for a point—the number of bits per pixel.

Consider the attribute range for screen 1, which is 0-3.
In binary, 2 bits are required to represent a decimal
number as large as 3. For a screen mode with an
attribute range of 0-1, only 1 bit is needed to represent
these values. Mathematically, the number of bits per
pixel is equal to the log base 2 of the maximum
attribute available for that screen mode. This concept
is particularly important when using the paint tiling
feature. See "PAINT Statement" in the *BASIC
Reference* for more information.

Medium Resolution: There are 320 horizontal and
200 vertical points in medium resolution. Points are
numbered from left to right, top to bottom, starting
with zero. The upper left corner of the screen is point
0,0; the lower right corner is point 319,199. The

numbering method is just the opposite of the usual mathematical method for numbering coordinates. Medium resolution is set by a SCREEN 1 statement.

Medium resolution is unusual because of its color characteristics. When you put something on the screen in medium resolution, you can specify a color attribute number of $\emptyset$, 1, 2, or 3. The colors for these attributes are not fixed, as are the 16 colors in text mode. You select the color for attribute number $\emptyset$, which will be your background color. Then you select one of two "palettes" for the other three attributes by using the COLOR statement. A palette is a set of three actual colors to be associated with attributes 1, 2, and 3. If you change the palette with a COLOR statement, all the colors on the screen change to match the new palette.

You can still display text characters on the screen when you are in graphics mode. The size of the character display area is the same as in text mode; that is, 25 lines of 4$\emptyset$ characters. In medium resolution, the foreground is attribute 3, and the background is attribute $\emptyset$.

High Resolution: In high resolution there are 64$\emptyset$ horizontal and 2$\emptyset\emptyset$ vertical points. As in medium resolution, points are numbered starting with zero with the lower right corner point being 639,199. High resolution is set by the SCREEN 2 statement.

High resolution has only two colors: black and white. Black is always $\emptyset$ (zero), and white is always 1 (one).

When you display text characters in high resolution, you get 8$\emptyset$ characters per line. The foreground color attribute is 1 and the background color attribute is $\emptyset$. Characters are always white on black.

Specifying Coordinates: The graphic statements require information about where on the screen you want to draw. You give this information in the form of coordinates. Coordinates are generally in the form (x,y), where x is the horizontal position, and y is the vertical position. This form is known as *absolute form* and refers to the actual coordinates of the point on the screen, without regard to the last point referenced.

There is another way to show coordinates, known as *relative form*. Using this form you tell BASIC where the point is, relative to the last point referenced. This form looks like:

```
STEP (xoffset,yoffset)
```

You indicate inside the parentheses the *offset* in the horizontal and vertical directions from the last point referenced.

Initially, (after SCREEN 1, SCREEN 2, WIDTH or CLS) the "last point referenced" is the point in the middle of the screen; that is (16Ø,1ØØ) for medium resolution, or (32Ø,1ØØ) for high resolution. Later statements change the last point referenced. What each graphics statement sets as the last point referenced is indicated in the discussion of that statement in the *BASIC Reference*.

> **Note:** In BASIC 2.Ø and later releases, images defined with coordinates that are out of range are clipped so that only points plotted within the boundaries of the window are visible.

This example shows the use of both forms of coordinates:

```
1ØØ SCREEN 1
11Ø PSET (2ØØ,1ØØ)      'absolute form
12Ø PSET STEP (1Ø,-2Ø) 'relative form
```

This sets two points on the screen. Their actual coordinates are (2ØØ,1ØØ) and (21Ø,8Ø).

Appendixes

Contents

Appendix A. BASIC Disk Input and Output

This appendix describes procedures and special considerations for using disk input and output. It contains lists of the commands and statements that are used with disk files, and explanations of how to use them. Several sample programs are included to help clarify the use of data files on disk. If you are new to BASIC or if you're getting disk-related errors, read through these procedures and program examples to make sure you're using all the disk statements correctly.

You may also want to refer to the IBM Personal Computer *Disk Operating System* (DOS manual) for other information on handling disks and disk files.

> **Note:** Most of the information in this appendix about program files and sequential files applies to cassette I/O as well. However, the cassette cannot be opened in random mode.

Specifying Filenames

Filenames for disk files must conform to DOS naming conventions in order for BASIC to be able to read them. See "Naming Files" in Chapter 3 to be sure you are specifying your disk files correctly.

Commands for Program Files

The commands you can use with your BASIC program files are listed below. For more detailed information on any of these commands, see the *BASIC Reference*.

CHAIN	NAME
KILL	RUN
LOAD	SAVE
MERGE	

Disk Data Files - Sequential and Random I/O

Two types of disk data files can be created and accessed by a BASIC program: sequential files and random access files.

Sequential Files

Sequential files are easier to create than random files, but are limited in flexibility and speed when it comes to accessing the data. The data that is written to a sequential file is stored sequentially, one item after another, in the order that it is sent. Each item is read back in the same way, from the first item in the file to the last item.

The statements and functions used with sequential files are:

CLOSE	LOF
EOF	OPEN
INPUT #	PRINT #
INPUT$	PRINT # USING
LINE INPUT #	WRITE #
LOC	

Creating and Accessing a Sequential File

To create a sequential file and access the data in it, include the following steps in your program:

1. Open the file for output or append using the OPEN statement.

2. Write data to the file using the PRINT #, WRITE #, or PRINT # USING statements.

3. To access the data in the file, you must close the file (using CLOSE) and reopen it for input (using OPEN).

4. Use the INPUT # or LINE INPUT # statements to read data from the sequential file into the program.

These steps are shown in PROGRAM1.

```
10 REM PROGRAM1 - SEQUENTIAL FILES
20 OPEN "DATA" FOR OUTPUT AS #1 'STEP 1
30 FOR I=1 TO 1040 PRINT #1,I 'STEP 2
50 NEXT
60 CLOSE 'STEP 3
70 OPEN "I",#1,"DATA"
80 IF EOF(1) THEN CLOSE:END
90 INPUT #1,A   'STEP 4
100 PRINT A
110 GOTO 80
```

Notice the two ways of writing the OPEN statement in
line 2∅ and line 7∅. See "OPEN Statement" in the
BASIC Reference for details of the syntax of each form
of OPEN.

In line 8∅ the EOF function tests for end of file. This
prevents an **Input past end** error. The end of file is
indicated by a special character in the file. This
character has ASCII code 26 (hex 1A). Therefore, you
should not put a CHR$(26) in a sequential file.

A program that creates a sequential file can also write
formatted data to the disk with the PRINT # USING
statement. For example, the statement:

```
PRINT #1,USING "####.## ";A,B,C,D
```

can be used to write numeric data to disk without
explicit delimiters. The space at the end of the format
string separates the items in the disk file.

The LOC function, when used with a sequential file,
returns the number of records that have been written to
or read from the file since it was opened. (A record is a
128-byte block of data.)

The LOF function returns the number of bytes
allocated to the file. For files created by BASIC 1.1∅,
LOF will return a multiple of 128, rounding upward if
necessary. For files created outside BASIC (using
EDLIN, for example) and for files created by BASIC
2.0 and later releases, LOF returns the actual number
of bytes allocated.

Adding Data to a Sequential File

To add data to a sequential file residing on disk, you cannot simply open the file for output and start writing data. When you open a sequential file for output, you destroy its current contents. Instead, you should open the file for APPEND. See "OPEN Statement" in the *BASIC Reference* for details.

Random Files

Creating and accessing random files require more program steps than sequential files, but there are advantages to using random files. For instance, numbers in random files are usually stored on disk in binary formats, while numbers in sequential files are stored as ASCII characters. Therefore, in many cases random files require less space on disk than sequential files.

The biggest advantage to random files is that data can be accessed randomly; that is, anywhere on the disk. It is not necessary to read through all the information, as with sequential files. This is possible because the information is stored and accessed in distinct units called records, and each record is numbered.

Records can be any length up to 32767 bytes. The size of a record is not related to the size of a sector on the disk (512 bytes). BASIC automatically uses all 512 bytes in a sector for information storage. It does this by both blocking records and spanning sector boundaries (that is, part of a record can be at the end of one sector and the other part at the beginning of the next sector).

The statements and functions used with random files are:

CLOSE	OPEN
FIELD	PUT
GET	
LSET/RSET	

```
CVD                              MKD$
CVI                              MKI$
CVS                              MKS$
LOC
LOF
```

Creating a Random File

The following program steps are required to create a
random file:

1. Open the file for random access. The example that
   follows specifies a record length of 32 bytes. If the
   record length is omitted, the default is 128 bytes.

2. Use the FIELD statement to allocate space in the
   random buffer for the variables that will be written
   to the random file.

3. Use LSET or RSET to move the data into the
   random buffer. Numeric values must be made into
   strings when placed in the buffer. To do this, use
   the "make" functions: MKI$ to make an integer
   value into a string; MKS$ for a single-precision
   value; and MKD$ for a double-precision value.

4. Write the data from the buffer to the disk using the
   PUT statement.

These steps are shown in PROGRAM2.

> **Note:** Do not use a string variable that has been
> defined in a FIELD statement in an input statement
> or on the left side of an assignment (LET)
> statement. This causes the pointer for that variable
> to point into string space instead of the random file
> buffer.

Look at PROGRAM2. It writes to a random file the
information entered at the keyboard. Each time the

PUT statement is executed, a record is written to the file. The two-digit code that is input in line 3Ø becomes the record number.

```
10 REM PROGRAM2 - CREATE A RANDOM FILE
20 OPEN "DATAY" AS #1 LEN=32   'STEP 1
30 FIELD #1,20 AS N$, 4 AS A$, 8 AS P$   'STEP 2
40 INPUT "2-DIGIT CODE";CODE%
50 IF CODE%=99 THEN CLOSE: END
60 INPUT "NAME";X$
70 INPUT "AMOUNT";AMT
80 INPUT "PHONE";TEL$: PRINT
90 LSET N$=X$   'STEP 3
100 LSET A$=MKS$(AMT)   'STEP 3
110 LSET P$=TEL$   'STEP 3
120 PUT #1,CODE%   'STEP 4
130 GOTO 40
```

Accessing a Random File

The following program steps are required to access a random file:

1. Open the file for random access.

2. Use the FIELD statement to allocate space in the random buffer for the variables that will be read from the file.

> **Note:** In a program that performs both input and output on the same random file, you can usually use just one OPEN statement and one FIELD statement.

3. Use the GET statement to move the desired record into the random buffer.

4. The data in the buffer can now be accessed by the program. Numeric values must be converted back to numbers using the "convert" functions: CVI for integers; CVS for single-precision values; and CVD for double-precision values.

These steps are shown in PROGRAM3.

PROGRAM3 accesses the random file that was created in PROGRAM2. When the two-digit code is entered at the keyboard, the information associated with that code is read from the file and displayed.

```
10 REM PROGRAM3 - ACCESS A RANDOM FILE
20 OPEN "DATAY" AS #1 LEN=32   'STEP 1
30 FIELD #1,20 AS N$, 4 AS A$, 8 AS P$ 'STEP 2
40 INPUT "2-DIGIT CODE";CODE%
50 IF CODE%=99 THEN CLOSE: END
60 GET #1, CODE%  'STEP 3
70 PRINT N$ 'STEP 4
80 PRINT USING "$$###.##";CVS(A$)   'STEP 4
90 PRINT P$
100 GOTO 40
```

With random files, the LOC function returns the current record number. The current record number is the latest one used in a GET or PUT statement. For example, the statement

```
IF LOC(1)>50 THEN END
```

ends program execution if the current record number in file #1 is higher than 5Ø.

Appendix B. Memory Information

This appendix contains information relating to BASIC's
memory, including a memory map and details on the
storage of variables, the keyboard buffer, and the
search order for adapters.

See the IBM Personal Computer *Technical Reference*
manual for technical information not presented in this
manual or the *BASIC Reference.*

Memory Map

This is a memory map for Disk and Advanced BASIC. DOS and the BASIC extensions are not present for Cassette BASIC. Addresses are in the hexadecimal form SEGMENT:OFFSET.

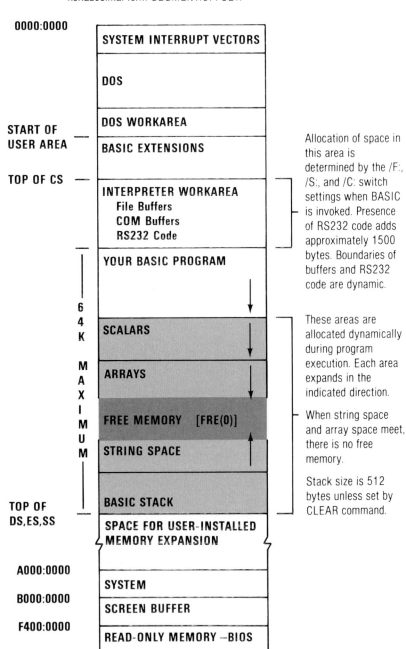

0000:0000

SYSTEM INTERRUPT VECTORS

DOS

DOS WORKAREA

START OF USER AREA —

BASIC EXTENSIONS

TOP OF CS —

INTERPRETER WORKAREA
File Buffers
COM Buffers
RS232 Code

Allocation of space in this area is determined by the /F:, /S:, and /C: switch settings when BASIC is invoked. Presence of RS232 code adds approximately 1500 bytes. Boundaries of buffers and RS232 code are dynamic.

YOUR BASIC PROGRAM

64K MAXIMUM

SCALARS

ARRAYS

These areas are allocated dynamically during program execution. Each area expands in the indicated direction.

FREE MEMORY   [FRE(0)]

STRING SPACE

When string space and array space meet, there is no free memory.

TOP OF DS,ES,SS —

BASIC STACK

Stack size is 512 bytes unless set by CLEAR command.

SPACE FOR USER-INSTALLED MEMORY EXPANSION

A000:0000

SYSTEM

B000:0000

SCREEN BUFFER

F400:0000

READ-ONLY MEMORY —BIOS

How Variables Are Stored

Scalar variables are stored in BASIC's data area as follows:

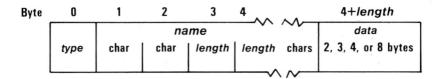

| type | name | | | | | data |

type   identifies the type of variable:

      2   integer
      3   string
      4   single-precision
      8   double-precision

name   is the name of the variable. The first two characters of the name are stored in bytes 1 and 2. Byte 3 tells how many more characters are in the variable name. These additional characters are stored starting at byte 4.

        Note that this means any variable name takes up at least three bytes. A one- or two-character name occupies exactly three bytes; an x character name occcupies $x+1$ bytes.

data   follows the name of the variable, and can be two, three, four, or eight bytes long (as described by *type*). The value returned by the VARPTR function points to this data.

For string variables, *data* is the *string descriptor*:

- The first byte of the string descriptor contains the length of the string ($\emptyset$ to 255).

- The last two bytes of the string descriptor contain the address of the string in BASIC's data space (the offset into the default segment). Addresses are stored with the low byte first and the high byte second, so:

  - The second byte of the string descriptor contains the low byte of the offset.
  - The third byte of the string descriptor contains the high byte of the offset.

For numeric variables *data* contains the actual value of the variable:

- Integer values are stored in two bytes, with the low byte first and the high byte second.

- Single-precision values are stored in four bytes in BASIC's internal floating point binary format.

- Double-precision values are stored in eight bytes in BASIC's internal floating point binary format.

Keyboard Buffer

Characters typed on the keyboard are saved in the keyboard buffer until they are processed. Up to 15 characters can be held in the buffer; if you try to type more than 15 characters, the computer beeps.

INKEY$ reads only one character from the keyboard buffer even if there are several characters pending there. INPUT$ can be used to read multiple characters; however, if the requested number of characters is not already present in the buffer, BASIC waits until enough characters are typed.

The system keyboard buffer can be cleared by the following lines of code:

```
DEF SEG=0: POKE 1050, PEEK(1052)
```

This technique can be used, for example, to clear the buffer before you ask the user to "press any key."

Search Order for Adapters

The printers associated with LPT1:, LPT2:, and LPT3: are assigned when you switch your computer on. The system looks for printer adapters in a particular sequence; the first printer adapter found becomes LPT1:; the second adapter (if one exists) becomes LPT2:; and the third (if it exists) becomes LPT3:. The search order is as follows:

1. An IBM Monochrome Display and Parallel Printer Adapter
2. A Parallel Printer Adapter
3. A Parallel Printer Adapter that has been modified to change its base address

If a printer was rerouted using the MODE command from DOS, the change is effective in BASIC as well.

The communication devices COM1: and COM2: are assigned in a manner similar to printers. Their search order is:

1. An Asynchronous Communications Adapter
2. A modified Asynchronous Communications Adapter

Switching Displays

If you have both the IBM Color/Graphics Monitor Adapter and the IBM Monochrome Display and Parallel Printer Adapter in your IBM Personal Computer, the one BASIC normally writes to is the Monochrome Display. However, you can switch from one display to the other from BASIC by using the following code:

```
10 ' switch to monochrome adapter
20 DEF SEG = 0
30 POKE &H410, (PEEK(&H410) OR &H30)
40 SCREEN 0
50 LOCATE ,,1,12,13
```

```
10 ' switch to color adapter
20 DEF SEG = 0
30 POKE &H410, (PEEK(&H410) AND &HCF) OR &H10
40 SCREEN 1,0,0,0
50 SCREEN 0
60 WIDTH 40
70 LOCATE ,,1,6,7
```

Note: When you use this technique, the screen you are switching *to* is cleared. Keep in mind that you may need to keep track of the cursor location independently for each display.

Index

Special Characters

A

B

or, exclusive 3-28
order of execution 3-32
output file mode A-5
output, formatting 3-22
output, standard 2-6
overscan 3-48

Q

Quick Reference iii

R

P

S

S: switch 2-7
SAMPLES program 2-29
screen 3-47
    use of 3-46
screen displays 3-46
screen or viewport, redefine
  coordinates viii
screen output 2-6
SCRN: 3-38
scrolling 3-47
search order for adapters B-5
semantics iii
sequential files A-4
SHELL ix
SHELL statement 2-9
single precision 3-12
soft keys 2-15
sound 1-3
spaces 3-6
special characters 3-5
specification of files 3-39
specifying coordinates 3-51
stack segment 2-8
standard input device 2-6
standard output 2-6
standard output option 2-6
starting BASIC 2-3
statement iii
statements that allow paths
    CHAIN vi
    OPEN vi
stdin 2-6
stdout 2-6
STEP 3-52
string comparisons 3-27
string constants 3-8
string descriptor B-4
string expressions 3-34
string functions 3-34
string space 2-9

string variables 3-17, 3-18
style vi
subdirectories 3-42
subtraction 3-24
summary of changes v
switches 2-6, 2-7
switching displays B-6
syntax iii
syntax errors 2-28
SYSTEM command 2-4
system requirements
    Advanced 1-5
    Cassette 1-4
    Disk 1-5

T

Tab key 2-23
techniques, formatting
  output 3-22
text mode 3-47
tiling vi
time 1-5
time from midnight vii
time from System Reset vii
TIMER function vii
trapping vii
tree-structured
  directories 3-43
true 3-25, 3-27
true-false table 3-27
truncation of program
  lines 2-26
twos complement 3-30, 3-31
type-declaration
  characters 3-18
types of directories 3-42
    root directory 3-42
    subdirectories 3-42

U

user workspace 2-9
using a program 2-29

V

variables 3-17, 3-18, B-3
  declaring types 3-17
  naming 3-17
  storage of B-3
  type-declaration
   characters 3-18
  types of 3-17
versions line explained 1-3
versions of BASIC 1-3
VIEW vii, 1-6
VIEW statement viii
viewport (area), define within
  limits of screen viii

visual page
  See display pages

W

WINDOW vii, 1-6
WINDOW statement viii
word 2-19
workspace 2-9
  maximum 2-9
world coordinates vii
wrapping, line 2-21, 2-23

X

XOR 3-28

Reader's Comment Form

BASIC HANDBOOK   6361129
General Programming Information

Your comments assist us in improving the usefulness of our publication; they are an important part of the input used for revisions.

IBM may use and distribute any of the information you supply in any way it believes appropriate without incurring any obligation whatever. You may, of course, continue to use the information you supply.

Please do not use this form for technical questions regarding the IBM Personal Computer or programs for the IBM Personal Computer, or for requests for additional publications; this only delays the response. Instead, direct your inquiries or request to your authorized IBM Personal Computer dealer.

Comments:

Tape

Please do not staple

Tape

Fold here

BUSINESS REPLY MAIL

FIRST CLASS   PERMIT NO. 321   BOCA RATON, FLORIDA 33432

POSTAGE WILL BE PAID BY ADDRESSEE

IBM PERSONAL COMPUTER
SALES & SERVICE
P.O. BOX 1328-C
BOCA RATON, FLORIDA 33432

NO POSTAGE
NECESSARY
IF MAILED
IN THE
UNITED STATES

The Personal Computer
Hardware Reference Library

Reader's Comment Form

BASIC HANDBOOK 6361129
General Programming Information

Your comments assist us in improving the usefulness of
our publication; they are an important part of the input
used for revisions.

IBM may use and distribute any of the information you
supply in any way it believes appropriate without
incurring any obligation whatever. You may, of course,
continue to use the information you supply.

Please do not use this form for technical questions
regarding the IBM Personal Computer or programs for
the IBM Personal Computer, or for requests for
additional publications; this only delays the response.
Instead, direct your inquiries or request to your
authorized IBM Personal Computer dealer.

Comments:

Tape   Please do not staple   Tape

Fold here

BUSINESS REPLY MAIL
FIRST CLASS   PERMIT NO. 321   BOCA RATON, FLORIDA 33432

POSTAGE WILL BE PAID BY ADDRESSEE

IBM PERSONAL COMPUTER
SALES & SERVICE
P.O. BOX 1328-C
BOCA RATON, FLORIDA 33432

NO POSTAGE
NECESSARY
IF MAILED
IN THE
UNITED STATES

Reader's Comment Form

BASIC HANDBOOK   6361129
General Programming Information

Your comments assist us in improving the usefulness of
our publication; they are an important part of the input
used for revisions.

IBM may use and distribute any of the information you
supply in any way it believes appropriate without
incurring any obligation whatever. You may, of course,
continue to use the information you supply.

Please do not use this form for technical questions
regarding the IBM Personal Computer or programs for
the IBM Personal Computer, or for requests for
additional publications; this only delays the response.
Instead, direct your inquiries or request to your
authorized IBM Personal Computer dealer.

Comments:

Tape   Please do not staple   Tape

Fold here
....

BUSINESS REPLY MAIL
FIRST CLASS   PERMIT NO. 321   BOCA RATON, FLORIDA 33432

POSTAGE WILL BE PAID BY ADDRESSEE

IBM PERSONAL COMPUTER
SALES & SERVICE
P.O. BOX 1328-C
BOCA RATON, FLORIDA 33432

NO POSTAGE
NECESSARY
IF MAILED
IN THE
UNITED STATES

The Personal Computer
Hardware Reference Library

Reader's Comment Form

BASIC HANDBOOK   6361129
General Programming Information

Your comments assist us in improving the usefulness of
our publication; they are an important part of the input
used for revisions.

IBM may use and distribute any of the information you
supply in any way it believes appropriate without
incurring any obligation whatever. You may, of course,
continue to use the information you supply.

Please do not use this form for technical questions
regarding the IBM Personal Computer or programs for
the IBM Personal Computer, or for requests for
additional publications; this only delays the response.
Instead, direct your inquiries or request to your
authorized IBM Personal Computer dealer.

Comments:

Tape   Please do not staple   Tape

Fold here
. . . .

BOCA RATON, FLORIDA 33432
P.O. BOX 1328-C
SALES & SERVICE
IBM PERSONAL COMPUTER

POSTAGE WILL BE PAID BY ADDRESSEE

BUSINESS REPLY MAIL
FIRST CLASS   PERMIT NO. 321   BOCA RATON, FLORIDA 33432

NO POSTAGE
NECESSARY
IF MAILED
IN THE
UNITED STATES